Stories, Sayings

Scriptures to Encourage and Inspire

hugs

™

to
encourage
and
inspire

HOWARD BOOKS

Stories by
JOHN WILLIAM SMITH

Personalized Scriptures by
LEANN WEISS

Our purpose at Howard Books is to:

• *Increase faith* in the hearts of growing Christians
• *Inspire holiness* in the lives of believers
• *Instill hope* in the hearts of struggling people everywhere

Because He's coming again!

Published by Howard Books, a division of Simon & Schuster, Inc.
1230 Avenue of the Americas, New York, NY 10020
www.howardpublishing.com

Hugs to Encourage and Inspire © 1997 by Howard Books

The previous printing was catalogued as follows:
Library of Congress Cataloging-in-Publication Data
Hugs for the heart : stories, sayings, and scriptures to encourage and inspire.
p. cm.

ISBN: 978-1-4767-4799-6

1. Spiritual life—Christianity—Miscellanea. I. Howard Books
BV4513.H84 1997
248.4—dc21

97-683
CIP

34 33 32 31 30 29 28 27 26

HOWARD is a registered trademark of Simon & Schuster, Inc.

Manufactured in the United States of America

For information regarding special discounts for bulk purchases, please contact: Simon & Schuster Special Sales at 1-800-456-6798 or business@simonandschuster.com.

Stories by John William Smith, author of *My Mother's Favorite Song, My Mother Played the Piano*, and contributor to other *Hugs* books

Scriptures paraphrased by LeAnn Weiss, owner of Encouragemnt Company, Orlando, Florida

Edited by Philis Boultinghouse
Cover design by LinDee Loveland
Interior design by LinDee Loveland

contents

one

the
victorious
heart

*I*f I am for you, who can be against you? In all things, you are much more than a victorious conqueror through me. Nothing can stop me from loving you – not death or life, angels or demons, current circumstances or anything in the future. Know that nothing and no one in all of the entire world can separate you from my totally awesome and indescribable love.

Love always and unconditionally,
Your God of Victory

Romans 8:31–39

With tears staining your cheeks and pride swelling your heart, you smile for the cheering thousands. The TV cameras pan the audience until they finally focus on your proud family, who is cheering encouragement to you and telling all within earshot that you belong to them.

Most of us will never know the exhilaration of winning a gold medal at the Olympics. But in our imaginations, we've all proudly stood on that top platform . . .

If only it could be true.

Your world may be filled with challenges just as trying as those faced by top Olympic contenders, but no roaring crowds cheer you on, and no one offers you a gold medal for your valiant efforts to win this game called life.

But wait . . . if you listen closely, you might just hear the faint sound of cheering. And as you open your heart to the possibilities, the cheers will become louder and louder as you discover their source. Hebrews 12 says that we have a great cloud of witnesses surrounding us, cheering us to run with perseverance the race marked out for us. More than spectators, these witnesses are previous competitors, and they understand the sacrifices you're making and the pain you've endured.

And if you'll pan the crowd, you'll see your Father – he's the one leading the cheer. Arms raised, index finger extended, he's shouting to you, "You're number one! You're number one!" Beside him is your brother Jesus. He's turning to others in the crowd, excitedly telling all that you belong to him.

You are declared the winner!

The spirit, the will to win, and the will to excel are the things that endure. These qualities are so much more important than the events that occur.

—Vince Lombardi

"It doesn't matter how many times they score on you. I'm proud of you. I want you to go back out there and finish the game."

the winner

I was watching some little kids play soccer. These kids were only five or six years old, but they were playing a real game – a serious game – two teams, complete with coaches, uniforms, and parents. I didn't know any of them, so I was able to enjoy the game without the distraction of being anxious about winning or losing –

I wished the parents and coaches
could have done the same.

The teams were pretty evenly matched. I will just call them Team One and Team Two. Nobody scored in the first period. The kids were hilarious. They were clumsy and terribly inefficient. They fell over their own feet, they stumbled over the ball, they kicked at the ball and missed it – but they didn't seem to care.

They were having fun.

the victorious heart

In the second quarter, the Team One coach pulled out what must have been his first team and put in the scrubs, except for his best player who now guarded the goal. The game took a dramatic turn. I guess winning is important – even when you're five years old – because the Team Two coach left his best players in, and the Team One scrubs were no match for them. Team Two swarmed around the little guy who was now the Team One goalie. He was an outstanding athlete, but he was no match for three or four boys who were also very good. Team Two began to score.

The lone goalie gave it everything he had, recklessly throwing his body in front of incoming balls, trying valiantly to stop them. Team Two scored two goals in quick succession. It infuriated the young boy. He became a raging maniac – shouting, running, diving. With all the stamina he could muster, he covered the boy who now had the ball, but that boy kicked it to another boy twenty feet away, and by the time he repositioned himself, it was too late – they scored a third goal.

I soon learned who the goalie's parents were. They were nice, decent-looking people. I could tell that his dad had just come from the office – he still had his suit and tie on. They yelled encouragement to their son. I became totally absorbed, watching the boy on the field and his parents on the sidelines.

After the third goal, the little kid changed. He could see it was no use; he couldn't stop them. He didn't quit, but he became quietly desperate –

futility was written all over him.

His father changed too. He had been urging his son to try harder – yelling advice and encouragement. But then he changed. He became anxious. He tried to say that it was okay – to hang in there. He grieved for the pain his son was feeling.

After the fourth goal, I knew what was going to happen. I've seen it before. The little boy needed help so badly, and there was no help to be had. He retrieved the ball from the net and handed it to the referee – and then he cried. He just stood there while huge tears rolled down both cheeks. He went to his knees and put his fists to his eyes – and he cried the tears of the helpless and brokenhearted.

the victorious heart

When the boy went to his knees, I saw the father start onto the field. His wife clutched his arm and said, "Jim, don't. You'll embarrass him." But he tore loose from her and ran onto the field. He wasn't supposed to – the game was still in progress. Suit, tie, dress shoes, and all – he charged onto the field, and he picked up his son so everybody would know that this was his boy, and he hugged him and held him and cried with him. I've never been so proud of a man in my life.

He carried him off the field, and when he got close to the sidelines I heard him say, "Scotty, I'm so proud of you. You were great out there. I want everybody to know that you are my son."

"Daddy," the boy sobbed, "I couldn't stop them. I tried, Daddy, I tried and tried, and they scored on me."

"Scotty, it doesn't matter how many times they scored on you. You're my son, and I'm proud of you. I want you to go back out there and finish the game. I know you want to quit, but you can't. And, son, you're going to get scored on again, but it doesn't matter. Go on, now."

It made a difference – I could tell it did. When you're all alone, and you're getting scored on – and you can't stop them – it means a lot to know that it doesn't matter to those who love you. The little guy ran back on to the field – and they scored two more times –

but it was okay.

I get scored on every day. I try so hard. I recklessly throw my body in every direction. I fume and rage. I struggle with temptation and sin with every ounce of my being – and Satan laughs. And he scores again, and the tears come, and I go to my knees – sinful, convicted, helpless. And my Father – my Father rushes right out on the field – right in front of the whole crowd – the whole jeering, laughing world – and he picks me up, and he hugs me and he says, "John, I'm so proud of you. You were great out there. I want everybody to know that you are my son, and because I control the outcome of this game, I declare you –

The Winner."

reflections . . .

_____

_____

_____

_____

_____

_____

_____

_____

_____

_____

_____

_____

the forgiven heart

*G*ood News! Everyone who believes in me receives total forgiveness of sin through my name. There isn't *any* condemnation. Because of what I did at Calvary, you've been set free from the law of sin and death. Your record has been wiped clean. I forgive and forget!

Love,

Your Savior and Forgiving Jesus

Acts 10:43
Romans 8:1–2
Hebrews 10:17

"You are forgiven."

Just words? No – much more. The mere utterance of these three little words can free prisoners from guilt in an instant. Say the words quietly to yourself; then speak them boldly to needy souls around you. Graciously accepting the forgiveness freely given to us by God, we are compelled to become conduits of forgiveness for others.

Someone near you needs forgiveness today. You hold the power to free them. If the offense was committed against you, remember your own undeserved forgiveness; draw from that abundant supply and share what has been given you – it is not yours to hoard. If the offense is against someone

else, speak a word of testimony about God's
loving forgiveness and encourage actions that lead to
healing.

Forgiveness releases others from their indebtedness
to us and releases us from our indebtedness to them –
both freed to love.

You have been given a precious power. Receive and
give it generously and often.

Our God has a big eraser.

—Billy Zeoli

She reached out and took
me by the chin, and she
held my face right up to
hers and made me look
straight into her eyes.

the neighborhood moochers

When I was twelve, our family finances got so bad that we moved into a cabin in an old trailer park at the corner of Twelve Mile Road and Crooks Road. Originally, these cabins had been built as the precursors of motels – a place for travelers to spend the night. As the town had spread out around them and travelers no longer came that way, the cabins fell into disuse, so the owners decided to rent them out by the month. My dad operated a Standard Oil gas station right across the street, so it was a convenient place for us to live.

I soon made friends with another boy in the trailer park named Don. In most ways, we had little in common. We were drawn together by our age, physical proximity, our mutual poverty, and our love for baseball.

the forgiven heart

We were baseball fanatics. We played at every opportunity, and when we couldn't find a game, we played catch in the trailer park. When dark came, we would play catch near the office lights of the trailer park until the residents got tired of the noise of the ball splatting in our gloves and drove us off. Then we would go and peruse our baseball cards. We had hundreds of them. We knew the names, positions, batting averages, and ERAs of every Detroit Tiger player.

When the neighborhood kids played, it was sort of understood that we would take turns supplying a ball. But Don and I never took a turn because we never had a decent ball – and our friends constantly reminded us of that fact. They called us the

neighborhood moochers.

When we showed up to play, they would say, *"Here come the neighborhood moochers."* For those of you who may not know the word *moocher* – it's another way of calling a person a *bum* or *beggar*.

Don and I would go to the high school field and spend long hours on Saturday looking for stray balls. The ones we found were always in sorry condition. The stitches were frayed or loose, and the covers were torn. We tried to hide "a multitude of sins" with black electrical tape, but the results were very dissatisfying.

We began to talk about how great it would be to see the looks on our friends' faces if we showed up with a brand new ball – especially a *Reach*. That was the kind the Tigers played with. They had them at Montgomery Ward, but they were $2.75 and might as well have been $100. But we couldn't get it out of our minds or our conversation. We didn't like to be called *bums* or *moochers* by our friends. We would walk to Royal Oak and go to Montgomery Ward to look at the baseballs. We would pick up the display model and lovingly caress the smooth, white, horsehide cover, finger the flawless red stitching, admire the dark blue "Reach" printed on the side, and imagine ourselves hitting home runs and throwing blazing fast balls.

It would not have occurred to me to steal one –
at least not seriously.

My home life and religious training had created inhibitions far too deep for that. *But Don was not religious,* and the only reservations he had were limited to the possibilities of getting caught. He mentioned it often. I would not consider it. Then he made a suggestion that allowed me to rationalize my reserves. He said that *he* would actually steal the ball; I would only divert the sales clerk. I thought I could do that, so I went along –

but I knew better.

I did my job. I diverted the sales clerk by pretending to be interested in some article far away from the baseballs. Don had on a jacket, and he slipped the ball underneath his jacket and under his armpit and walked out of the store. In a couple of minutes, I followed. As I made my way up the stairs, I heard a familiar female voice call my name. I turned, and there stood Norma, a lady who went to church with us.

She asked me to come back down and talk to her. I didn't want to, but I went. She asked me what I was doing at the store. I was so flustered and nervous that I couldn't say anything. She told me that she was a store detective and that she had seen Don take the baseball and knew that I had helped him. I tried at first to explain the harmlessness of my involvement, but it was no use – I was just as guilty as Don, and

we both knew it.

There are no words to adequately describe all the feelings that poured over me in that single moment of time – in a rush, I thought about what this would mean to my family, the church, my friends. She told me to go and get Don and to bring him and the ball back.

Don was standing outside, flushed with excitement because we had *gotten away with it*. When I told him we hadn't, he wanted to run. He said no one could catch us, but

I knew there was no place
for me to run to.

I told him we had to go back. He wouldn't go – but he gave me the ball and said I could go back if I wanted to, and he took off.

Like a sheep to the slaughter, I went back. I told Norma that Don had run away. She said that she didn't care about him, but she just couldn't understand how I could do such a thing. *I didn't understand it either.* I

the forgiven heart

really didn't, because I didn't know much about sin and how it creeps up on a person, how it takes advantage of every weakness and exploits every desire until we find a way of doing it that doesn't seem so bad. We talked for a long time, and I cried – she did too. I wondered what she was going to do with me.

When we finished talking, she just sat sort of hunched over with her chin resting in her hand. She looked at me for a long time – like she was having trouble making up her mind. She finally straightened up and sighed, a great, big, long one – like she had been holding her breath for about ten minutes – which let me know she had made up her mind. She reached out and took me by my chin, and she held my face right up to hers and made me look straight into her eyes, and she said,

"Johnny, you go home,
and don't you ever let me catch you
in this store without your parents,
ever again.
This will stay
between the two of us."

the neighborhood moochers

I don't remember ever going back into Montgomery Ward ever again –

not even with my parents.

If they went there to shop, I made some excuse to stay outside – and I still don't shop at Montgomery Ward without looking over my shoulder for Norma. When I think of *forgiveness,* of the inexpressible delight there is in pardon, I think of that experience.

Now I have grown older and much more discreet about stealing baseballs. My justifications and rationalizations are much more elaborate. But it always ends up the same way. I hear a familiar voice calling my name, and that rush of confusion, guilt, and shame comes over me, because I know I am caught once again. I hear that voice say, "What are you doing in this store?" And at first I try to explain the harmlessness of my involvement. I give all the standard excuses, but it's no good –

we *both* know.
"Did you think you could get away with that?
When are you going to learn?
I saw you do it."

the forgiven heart

And then we talk, and I cry – so does he – and I wonder what he's going to do with me. It's not jail this time, not a criminal record, it's not my reputation or the church or even my family that I'm worried about – no, this is the big one – *I could go to hell for this!* He sits hunched over in his chair, his chin resting in his hands, and he looks at me with hurt in his eyes. But unlike Norma, he does not deliberate over what he will do with me. He made up his mind about that a long time ago – when he first planned to allow his Son to take the punishment that was coming to me.

He reaches out his hand and takes me by the chin, and he makes me look straight into his eyes, and he says –

"Johnny, I forgive you;
go home.
And don't you ever
let me catch you in this store again –
unless *I'm* with you."

reflections . . .

the humbled heart

*P*ractice humility toward one another. I oppose the proud. But I give my amazing grace to those who are humble.

Love,

Your God Who Is Gentle

and Humble in Heart

1 Peter 5:5

I'm going to tell you a secret that will make you feel a whole lot better about yourself. It's something you've allowed yourself to consider before . . . but not for very long.

The very essence of this secret will make you bristle, even though you know that accepting it will ease your mind, calm your spirit, and even whet your appetite for growth.

Are you ready? I know you can handle it, though not everyone can. Here goes: You are not always right.

I saw you smile, because you know I'm right – well, about this, anyway.

Trying to be right about everything is a load you cannot carry, and the cost is far more than you can afford.

The next time you look in the mirror, you may

want to remind yourself of this secret.

And I'll tell you another secret – admitting that

you're not always right makes you even more lovable

than you already are – if that's possible.

God created the world out of nothing, and so long as we are nothing, he can make something out of us.

—Martin Luther

I learned a lesson
from Gertrude.
I learned that I'm
not always right.

gertrude

My son Lincoln and I had been to the town of Frankenmuth, Michigan, to fish. He was about eleven at the time. The town is only about fifty miles from Flint, where we lived, and is nearly world famous for its breweries and for Zenders – a national monument to fried chicken and sauerbraten. It is much less well known for salmon fishing, but that's why we went there. The Clinton River is dammed there, and the Lake Huron salmon collect below the dam.

We drove over right after school, hoping to fish a couple of hours before dark. It was late fall. When we headed home, after a very successful trip, it was cold and dark. We were speeding along a narrow, twisting country road, when suddenly, my headlights revealed a white piscovey duck in the middle of the road. I can't imagine what it was doing in the road at that time of night. I thought ducks were like chickens and went to sleep as soon as it got dark – and this one should have. I was going much too fast to swerve, and there was no time to stop. I heard the sickening *whack* and *crunch* of the duck hitting the underside of the car repeatedly.

It isn't easy to explain my next action – in fact, it's a little embarrassing – but I have to try, or I can't tell the rest of the story. You need to know me personally, and you need to understand the way I was brought up. In my family –

> nothing was ever wasted –
> it was a sin to waste.

I turned around and went back to pick up the duck so we could take it home and eat it. It was lying in a heap, sprawled out in obvious death in the middle of ten thousand feathers. I pulled up alongside, reached out my door, picked up the duck, laid it on the floor behind my seat, and headed home once again. I was driving a compact car. It was an Opel with bucket seats.

Lincoln was very quiet as we drove, but completely alert. Normally, he would have been sound asleep after such a day, but the incident with the duck had totally captured his imagination. I noticed that he kept looking behind my seat. A few minutes later, he said,

"Dad, do ducks have souls?"

"No, Son, ducks don't have souls."

"What happens to a duck when it dies?"

"We eat it."

"I mean, where does it go?"

"It doesn't go anywhere. It just *isn't* anymore."

"Oh." He thought for a few minutes and then he said, "Dad, is it okay to pray for a duck?"

"I guess so, but why would you want to?"

"I feel sorry for it."

He lapsed into a thoughtful silence, and I assumed that he was praying. He kept his eyes on the duck, and a few minutes later he spoke again.

"Dad?"

"What, Son?"

"God just answered my prayer; that duck's alive."

"God doesn't do things like that anymore. The duck is dead."

A few minutes passed.

the humbled heart

"Dad? Why doesn't God do things like that any-more?"

"Because the age of miracles ceased when the apostle John died."

"Dad, are you sure of that? The duck is alive. I just saw it move."

"No, Son, the duck may have moved from the motion of the car, but that duck is not alive. I know you feel sorry for the duck, and I do, too, and I know you prayed for the duck; but we have to learn to accept bad things in life. *The duck is dead.* You heard it hit the car, didn't you?"

"Yes, but, Dad, the duck just moved again, and it's not the motion of the car. *It's looking right at me.*"

"Son, this has gone far enough. You mustn't allow your imagination to run away with you. I've told you that the duck is dead. *It is dead!* No amount of wishful thinking can bring it back. Trust me. I'm your father, and when *I* tell you that the duck is *dead,* you can believe me.

The – duck – is – dead!
Now, I don't want to hear any more

about that duck;
do you understand?"

"Yes, Sir."

"Quack."

"What was that noise?"

"I think it was the dead duck, Dad."

I turned around, and sure enough, there was the duck, standing up and looking rather puzzled by its new surroundings.

"Son," I said, "the age of miracles just started again, because that duck was dead!"

We took it home, fed it, found a marvelous place for it to stay – in our swimming pool, which was closed for the winter anyway – and we named her (I guess it was a her) Gertrude. About a month later we went back to Frankenmuth. We took Gertrude and released her as near to the spot where we had found her as possible and went on our way.

I learned a lesson from Gertrude the duck that day. I learned that I'm not always right. I learned that older isn't always wiser; I learned that sometimes we allow our presuppositions to override obvious facts; and I

the humbled heart

learned that if I insist on being right and won't even *listen* to another point of view, I might be forced to acknowledge my fallibility by a loud "Quack" of reality.

The next time you feel compelled to stand your ground, no matter the facts, just remember Gertrude the duck and relax a little. Learn the grace of laughing at yourself.

It really isn't so bad to admit that you're wrong –
once in a while.

reflections . . .

four

at the heart of grace

I saved you by grace through faith. You couldn't earn eternal life on your own. Your debt was too enormous. No works could ever begin to repay what my Son did for you. It's a lavish gift of grace from me to you.

Love,

Your God of Amazing Grace

Ephesians 2:8–9
Romans 8:32

You are at home watching an episode of *I Love Lucy*. Suddenly, there's a knock at the door. You're agitated at the interruption of your cultural exchange with the '50s, but you answer the door anyway.

And guess who's there? It's Ed McMahon! He's holding a gargantuan foam-board check with $10,000,000 scrawled across it in rolling script.

Your breathing accelerates; every nerve in your body tingles. You can hardly believe that you are suddenly free of the financial debt and worry that has burdened your life. "I don't deserve this," you whisper to yourself, "but this is great!"

Then the roar of an airplane flying overhead jolts you awake – it was only a dream.

Oh, but it's not a dream. It really did happen. You remember . . .

there was a knock at the door of your heart; you answered and met a man with nail scarred hands and feet. He held a bill in his hand, totaling your debt at an impossible sum. But remember . . . he tore it up and handed you the pieces; then he gave you his priceless grace instead.

Your breathing accelerated; every nerve in your body tingled. You could hardly believe that you were suddenly free from the debt of guilt and the fear of death that had plagued your whole life. "I don't deserve this," you whispered to yourself, and you were right – you don't.

The greatest surprise imaginable is not a sweepstakes bonanza – it's the gift of grace given by a holy God.

And now he plans to use your name and likeness to win others.

How magnificent is grace! How sweet are the promises! How sour is the past! How precious and broad is God's love! How petty and narrow are man's limitations! How refreshing is the Lord!

—Charles Swindoll

He smiled when I told him I would try to repay him some day. "Forget it," he said. "I'll get more than my money's worth telling this story over the next twenty-five years."

pinson mounds

It was Friday night. I had been to Jackson, Tennessee, with my date and was now returning to the college we attended in Henderson. As we approached the thriving metropolis of Pinson – a city of seventy-five souls, known worldwide for the *Pinson Mounds* (nothing to do with candy bars) – the car started pulling radically to the left, which could only mean one thing – another flat tire. I swerved quickly into a little roadside pullout sheltered by oak trees.

Now, the pullout wasn't such a bad place, especially in view of who I was with – and I never was one to cast aside lightly what had obviously been made available to me providentially. But eventually, I knew I was going to have to do something. Joan was very understanding,

at the heart of grace

but she had to be back in the dormitory by 10:30, or we would both have to stand trial before the D.C. – *Discipline Committee* – to explain our whereabouts on the night in question. I had already had the dubious honor, if not pleasure, of receiving a personal invitation to appear before this venerated and august group of sages on several previous occasions and had no desire for a *return engagement.*

Across the street from the pullout was a one-stall, combination repair shop, junk dealer, post office, hardware store, gas station, *you-name-it-we-got-it* place. It had closed before dark, but the owner/proprietor's house was next door. It was my only hope. There were no lights on, and it was obvious that they were in bed. I knocked timidly at first, but getting no response and being rather desperate, I banged loudly. This aroused the dog, who, from the sound he made, must have resembled King Kong – but, fortunately, he was chained. I began to hear the angry mutterings and rumblings of someone who obviously had a deep resentment toward this unwarranted disruption of his nocturnal bliss.

A light went on, the door opened slightly, and then he appeared. His hair was disheveled, his pants, hastily thrown on over long-handled underwear – which also served as his night-time attire – hung by one suspender. He was barefoot, his eyes were half-open, and when he opened the door, he had a most unpleasant expression on his face.

"Good evening, Sir," I said in my most cheerful, polite, and deferential tone.

"Good *morning* you mean," he said – neither cheerfully, politely, nor deferentially. "It's got to be after midnight – Whadayawant?"

"I'm very sorry to inconvenience you, Sir, but you see, I have a problem."

"Don't give me that *inconvenience* rubbish – everybody's got problems, Sonny – even me," he said as he looked sourly and suspiciously at me.

"Oh really?" I said. "I'm sorry to hear that, but you see, I have a flat tire."

"Come back tomorrow." He started to close the door.

"But I can't do that," desperation was edging into my voice. "I'm from Freed-Hardeman, over in

Henderson, and my girl has to be in the dorm by 10:30, and if I don't get her there, we'll be in big trouble." I tried to slide my foot forward so he couldn't close the door.

"Put your spare tire on."

"Well, Sir, that's another problem. I don't *exactly* have a spare tire."

He emitted a long sigh of resignation and hopelessness – the kind of sigh that every parent learns all too quickly.

"Where's your car, Sonny?"

"Right over there behind those oaks," I said, as I pointed across the road.

"Okay. You go get the tire off and bring it over, and I'll fix it."

"Yes sir," I said enthusiastically. "But – well – actually, you see, I don't *exactly* have a jack either."

"Don't *exactly* have a jack? Son, either you have a jack or you don't have a jack. What *exactly* do you have? Do you have one *approximately?* Oh, forget it. There's one in that shed there beside the shop. Don't let Old Walt scare you; he's chained up. He sounds real fierce, but he's never *exactly* hurt anybody – seriously."

"Say, thanks a lot. You – uh – you wouldn't happen to have a lug wrench would you?"

"Oh, Lord, why me?" he muttered under his breath. "Yeah, there should be one in there with the jack," he said out loud. "Anything else you don't *exactly* have?"

"No, Sir," I said confidently, "that ought to just about do it."

It turned out that the jack was just about a foot from the end of Old Walt's chain, which looked very fragile. Old Walt was a bit much. He looked like a cross between a grizzly bear and a mountain lion, and he acted as if he hadn't eaten in six weeks. He absolutely terrified me – lunging so hard against the end of his chain that he actually dragged his house, to which the chain was attached, behind him. His snarl began somewhere in the pit of his stomach, and by the time it came ripping, hissing, rattling, and roaring out his throat, it sounded like an avalanche. His eyes looked like laser beams, he had foam around his mouth, saliva dripped from his jaws, and when he snapped and ground his huge teeth, sparks flew. Old Walt was the original and archetypal *Junk Yard Dog.* I found a piece of rope, lassoed the jack, and dragged it close enough to me that I could grab it and run.

As I took the lug nuts off, I placed them in the hubcap for safe keeping. It was totally dark where the car was, and I had been too ashamed to ask for a flashlight, which I didn't *exactly* have either. The rim was rusted tightly to the drum, and I had to kick it with all my might to break it loose. When it finally flew off, it hit the edge of the hubcap and scattered the lug nuts in every direction, mostly under the car. I could only find one because the ground was about three inches deep in oak leaves. To make matters worse, I also discovered that I could *see through* my tire. It was absolutely ruined, and so was the inner tube. When I crossed the road again, tire in hand, I was simply wretched. My benefactor was in the garage.

"I don't think this tire is any good," I said apologetically. "You don't *happen* to have one do you?"

"I don't *happen* to have nothin', Sonny. What I got here, I got *on purpose,* and I do have one." He rummaged around and eventually found a pretty decent tire.

"I could let you have this one for five bucks."

"Do you have one any less expensive? I don't *exactly* have five dollars," I said.

"How *much* less expensive? Maybe I could let it go for three," he said.

"I don't *exactly* have three either."

"Well, how much *exactly* do you have?" he said with exasperation.

"Well, if you put it in *exact* terms, I reached in my front pocket and counted out the change, "I have thirty-five cents," I said hopefully.

At that very moment, Joan appeared. She had grown tired of waiting and had come to see if I was making any progress.

Joan was very, very pretty.

"Who in the world is this?" he said, with a whistle and obvious admiration in his voice.

"Oh, this is Joan; she's my date."

He looked appreciatively at Joan.

"You sure must be some *talker*, Sonny. She sure didn't go with you for your *looks*, your *money*, your *brains*, or your *car.*"

at the heart of grace

A pretty girl does wonders to men. In the presence of Joan, his whole attitude changed. He became gracious, kind, even cheerful – he forgot his inconvenience. He *gave* me the tire, found a tube, patched it, found some spare lug nuts, and helped me put it on. He even invited me to stop by and visit with him on my next trip to Jackson –

if I brought Joan.

He smiled when I told him I would try to repay him some day. "Oh," he said, "that's okay. Forget it. I'll get more than my money's worth telling this story over the next twenty-five years. But nobody will believe it."

It wasn't until I got back to my room that I began to realize that I had just learned something about *salvation by grace*. I had learned what it means to be totally helpless, to have *absolutely nothing* in your hands but your need, and to receive a *gift* that is offered to you cheerfully and at personal cost –

a gift you can never repay.

reflections . . .

five

the selfless heart

*D*on't be selfish or self-seeking in anything you do. Instead of being self-promoting, be humble and consider others more important than yourself in all you do and say. Encourage one another, and build each other up.

Love,

Jesus

Philippians 2:3
1 Thessalonians 5:11

When was the last time

you felt really warm and loved? Think about it. It was probably the last time someone went out of their way to do or say something nice to you – unasked, out-of-the-blue, just because – something that made you feel valued and appreciated.

Though you've heard it a thousand times before, the essence of love is *giving*. Give of yourself and of your time; give surprise gifts and encouraging words. Take your spouse on a date and focus all your attention on your chosen one. Gather your family around the kitchen table and initiate an appreciation session, where each member shares positive things about the others. Take a friend to lunch just to remind him or her that you cherish your relationship.

Giving is the spark that ignites the fires of love. You have the power to start a blazing fury of selfless love.

Maturity begins to grow
when you can sense
your concern for others
outweighing your
concern for yourself.

—John McNaughton

I was so dumb — so lost in my own world, my own happiness, feelings, and pleasures — my own needs and wants — that I didn't know anybody else had any.

winter of our discontent

"Now is the winter of our discontent
made glorious summer by this son of York."
—Shakespeare, *King Lear*

It was spring at last. Judi was pregnant – in fact –
she was *extremely* pregnant – it was our first child. We
lived in a very small apartment in Mount Clemens,
Michigan. It was 1964. It had been *a long, hard winter.*
All along the roadways were great mounds of soot-
blackened, grimy, slowly melting snow, standing as
bleak reminders of the cold and lonely months behind
us. The departed snow left a newly naked and embarrassed landscape, covered with an uninviting array of
dead, brown weeds and grass, sprinkled with scattered bits
of blown, discarded trash that had been conveniently

the selfless heart

hidden until now. Spring didn't look like the *beginning* of something –

it looked like the *end*.

If I say that this happened in the winter of '64, "winter" sounds like an isolated entity – like saying "senior year." *A Michigan winter is not a single thing.* It is a multifaceted, amalgamation of things that get all mixed up and twisted together. The event that I am about to record was not a single event; it was the culmination of a thousand events, some so infinitely small that neither of us noticed or remembered them – but they happened – they had been happening since we began our courtship and marriage.

We only had one car, which I used in my work. I was busy in my job – I left early and came home late. I went places, met people, had lunch, hunted, fished, and played golf. Judi was home alone every day, *and she was pregnant.* I emphasize her pregnancy because *no man has ever experienced it or understands it* (few have even tried – understanding it, I mean) and because *pregnancy is such a unique thing* – especially the first one. We knew very few people – she had no transportation and no place to go.

The winter had been made even longer by the fact that we had no money and therefore could not *buy* our way out of the oppressive isolation that had settled over us. There were no shopping trips, no movies, no evenings out.

We had been married long enough for the new and the curiosity to wear off, but not long enough to be comfortable with each other or our vanished, unrealistic expectations.

We had lost the world of our wishes –
but we had not replaced it
with one of our hopes.
It had been a very long winter!

Even the advent of spring hadn't been much help. Gray, overcast skies continued to depress, temperatures made promises that were never kept – and still no money.

Finally, we woke up one Friday morning to sunny, encouraging skies. As I left the house, I mentioned quite casually that if things went well at work and I got off early, we might drive up the river road to Charlevoix and have dinner.

"Oh, could we?" There was great expectation in her voice, but I wasn't paying attention.

Things went unexpectedly well at work, and by 11:30 I was finished. An unexpected sale had put some unexpected dollars in my pocket, and when my fishing buddy, Larry, called and told me that the perch were running in the Clinton River, my unexpected expectations ran totally out of control.

I didn't deliberately break my word to Judi – in some ways that would have been more honorable.

I did something worse –
I forgot her.

I broke all speed records getting home – locked up all four wheels and skidded to a stop in a cloud of dust in the driveway – ran into the house and yelled, "Hi, I'm home," as I yanked off my tie and unbuttoned my shirt, preparing to change into fishing clothes.

"What are you doing?"

It wasn't a challenge; it was a pleading question, but I didn't hear *the pleading* –

I just heard the question.

"I'm going fishing with Larry; the perch are running in the Clinton River."

I hadn't seen her yet, but now she came into the bedroom. She had her hair all done up, and she was dressed in her only Sunday "pregnant" dress –

but I never noticed.

"Oh," she said. Hurt and disappointment were in the "Oh"–

but I didn't hear her pain.

"Could you fix me a thermos of tea and a couple of sandwiches?"

"Sure," she said. "How long will you be gone?" There was *longing* in the question, but I was totally occupied with my preparations.

"Oh, probably till dark – depends on how good it is."

She was standing just inside the door as I rushed past, fishing rods in one hand, lunch in the other.

"Have a good time," she said, and although it was sincere, there was pain in it; but the pain escaped me – at least it escaped my consciousness.

"I'm sure I will," I said. *"You have a good time too."*

the selfless heart

"Sure," she said.

I put the rods in the trunk and the lunch on the seat. I started the motor and started to back up, but something was nagging at me. I went over a list of the things I would need, but that wasn't it. I had the eerie feeling that I had forgotten something, that something was missing, so I got out and went back inside to look.

She was standing right where I had left her – just inside the door – eyes wide open and huge tears rolling down both cheeks. She wasn't shaking or sobbing; she was just standing there – hands at her sides, eyes wide open, tears running down – looking at me.

"Honey, what's wrong?" I was so dumb – so lost in my own world, my own happiness, feelings, and pleasures – my own needs and wants – *that I didn't know anybody else had any.*

"You never have time for me."

She didn't yell, didn't even raise her voice; it would have been easier if she had. It was just a quiet statement of truth that left me convicted and heartsick. Everything just sort of went out of me – I felt lost, empty, and sick all at the same time. I just stood there

– I had no words for the feeling that *the entire founda-tion of my life* had just been destroyed, taken right out from under me, leaving me dangling. Her words seemed to hang in the air –

"You never have time for me."

I didn't know that I was *supposed* to have time for her – or for anybody else for that matter – unless it served some selfish purpose. Again, I want you to see that I wasn't mean or vicious. I wasn't one to speak harshly or be abusive; I was simply and totally self-centered – so much so that –

I didn't even know it.

What does a man do with a crying wife? I went fishing – not with Larry, but with Judi – but my heart wasn't in the fishing. I don't even remember if we caught anything. We sat on the riverbank, and we held hands and talked – but not much – I wasn't ready. We ate the sandwiches and drank the tea, and once, she took my hand and placed it on her extended tummy – "Feel that?" she said.

"Wow!" I said.

"That's your son kicking around in there."

the selfless heart

It was the beginning – no it actually wasn't – beginnings are hard to pin down. It had begun long ago, somewhere in the dim recesses of my childhood. Perhaps it was the beginning of awareness – an awareness of other people, of what a marriage is supposed to be. I lay awake late that night – long after I heard the slow, steady breathing that meant she was asleep – with all kinds of new thoughts buzzing around in my head. I didn't know it, but *the winter of our discontent* was over – it was becoming the spring of promise, because

I was becoming a man.

Read the following passage slowly – very slowly – and with care –

"When I was a child, I used to speak as a child,
think as a child, reason as a child;
when I became a man,
I did away with childish things. . . .
But now abide faith, hope, love,
these three;
but the greatest of these
is love."
—1 Corinthians 13:11, 13

winter of our discontent

The winter of our discontent had been created by my selfishness – by my refusal to put my egocentric childhood behind me and grow into the man that God intended me to be so that I could begin to learn the meaning of love. The first duty of a husband or wife is *to grow up – to put childhood aside –*

> to become a man or woman –
> and to think of others.

reflections . . .

_____

_____

_____

_____

_____

_____

_____

_____

_____

_____

_____

_____

reminding
the heart

I want you to think about whatever is true. Think about things that are noble or right . . . things that are pure and lovely. Reflect upon admirable qualities and memories. Remember whatever is excellent or praiseworthy.

Love,

Your God of Every

Good and Perfect Gift

Philippians 4:8

You may not realize it, but

you are a rich person. Yes, *you!* You possess a huge vault
brimming with treasure, and you can withdraw assets
from this vault whenever you want – at absolutely no cost.

Where is this vault? It is inside the caverns of your
heart and mind. And what treasure resides there? *Memories.*

Memories are pictures of past events and people that
can powerfully affect your present and future. There are
those funny memories that make you laugh, even now,
though the incident may have taken place years ago.

Then there are those embarrassing memories that
flash through your mind at the oddest times, even
causing you to blush.

But there are certain kinds of memories
that glisten like diamonds. They remind you
that your life is rich with meaning and
purpose – that you matter to other

people and that other people matter to you.

Memories of special moments when love was
exchanged and cherished, when a significant relationship
took a big step forward, when delicious laughter cheered
your soul – these precious memories are all waiting for you
to pick them up, dust them off, and bring them to life
once again.

So when your heart is heavy or you're feeling all
alone, open the door . . . go ahead. Dig in. Make all the
withdrawals you want. You can't deplete the supply. In
fact, you may find that you are so rich you can loan
some of your wealth to others.

Oops, look out – you got a little gold dust
on your smile.

Enjoy yourself. These
are the good old days
you are going to miss
in ten years.

—unknown

They say you
can't save time
in a bottle – but
maybe you can.

time in a bottle

I woke up thinking about Fred Alexander. I couldn't figure out why. I've only seen Fred two or three times in the last thirty years. I lay there in bed and puzzled over it – did I have a dream about Fred that I couldn't remember? And then it came to me. I don't know how or why,

but it came to me.

We were at Michigan Christian College, and it was the spring of 1961. The school year had just ended. Finals were over, dorm rooms were empty, annuals were signed, cars were loaded, and goodbyes were said – we were going home. There were seven or eight of us left, as I remember it – Wayne Baker, John Losher, Jim Began, Bill Hall, Bob Forrester, John Whitwell, Gary . . . something, myself, and Fred Alexander.

We were the only ones left.

reminding the heart

We met in one of the now empty, bare, sterile dorm rooms. Fred Alexander was a school administrator of sorts, and he also served as the chorus director. He and his wife, Claudette, were much loved by the students.

We met by design – one of the boys had specifically set up the meeting and had invited Fred. We met to say goodbye – in some final, official, personal way. Each of us tried to say something important – something significant – we tried to find an expression for what was in our hearts – to give vent to the love, the sorrow, the loneliness that we felt.

We were so aware of time.

Until now, we had not been aware at all. We had played football and basketball in the long, fall afternoons – we had eaten in the cafeteria, gone to chapel, dated girls, talked late at night about unimportant things, gone to Red Knapps for hamburgers, played Spades and Hearts, crammed for tests, bragged about our adventures, and fooled away endless hours canoeing on the Clinton River and visiting Yates Cider Mill – all with no consciousness of time – but we were conscious now – painfully so. The year was over. Time does not need consciousness to pass. Things had changed without notice –

they would never be the same.

The meeting was awkward; we were embarrassed. We were only boys, and we were experiencing things for the first time, so we had no words. Although I was older than the other boys, I was as lost as any of them, maybe more so, because growing up had come very slowly to me.

Finally, we joined hands in a circle – and we prayed. And as we prayed, we began to cry – first one – then another – finally all. It was a new experience for some of us. When we finished our prayer, we shook hands – then, awkwardly, we embraced each other –

and then it was time to go.

We asked Fred if he had something to share with us. His eyes were red too – I don't think he was much used to crying either. His voice shook, but I remember what he said.

"If I could have any wish right now, I'd wish that I could take this moment and put it in a jar – and put a lid on it, so each of us could hold it. And every now and then – wherever we go – at those special times when life is cruel – we'd open the jar and let a little bit of what is in this room out – and we would remember the experience of loving and being loved –

and it would make us whole again."

They say you can't save time in a bottle – but maybe you can. Maybe Fred was on to something.

Maybe you *can* save time in a bottle.
Maybe you *can* preserve the love.
Maybe remembering is as good as being there.
No, you can't *go* back, but you can *be* back.
Maybe you can save time in a bottle.

Memories are sustaining things. They give meaning and purpose not only to the past but to the present – and they bring hope for the future.

Reach up and take that jar off the shelf. Open the lid slowly – be careful not to let too much escape at once. Savor every aroma and draw strength for today

from the blessings of the past.

reflections . . .

_____

_____

_____

_____

_____

_____

_____

_____

_____

_____

_____

_____

the courageous heart

*B*e full of strength and courage. Do not be terrified; do not be discouraged. I will be with you wherever you go.

Love,

Your God of

Strength and Courage

Joshua 1:9

Would you describe your-
self as a person of courage?

Probably not.

Your image of courage has been shaped by
television and movies. Courage is John Wayne
risking his life to insure justice for the underdog
who is losing his ranch to a scheming card shark.
It's Superwoman flying to rescue a helpless child
from a burning building. Or perhaps it's Will
Smith saving the world from aliens who plan
to destroy us and confiscate our natural
resources.

Make-believe courage is hard to live
up to. But real courage in real life
may describe you to a tee. It takes
courage to care about family

and friends enough to get involved with their struggles. It takes courage to complete what you start. It takes courage to confront weakness in your own life and in the lives of those you love so that needed changes can take place. It takes courage to confess that your thoughtless words or negligent actions have hurt someone you love. Quite simply, it takes courage to live each day with integrity.

You may not describe yourself as a person of courage, but look again – you may discover courageous feats of kindness or heroic manifestations of unconditional love.

Say, would you like to be in a movie?

Courage is fear that
has said its prayers.

—from
One Day at a Time in Al-Anon

He was conscious of two opposing things simultaneously.
First, he wished he had not
made a public issue out of
this, and second, he was glad
he had and he didn't care.

following Jesus

*"If any man would come after me,
let him . . . take up his cross
and follow me."*
—Mark 8:34

He was a ninth-grade English teacher, and he was a Christian. He was a large man, with an athletic and intimidating physique. The school he taught in was located on the *bad side of town,* and the kids were loud, tough, crude, vulgar, and unappreciative. Although his students liked him well enough, they thought he was an odd duck because he really believed that education was important and therefore took his duties much too seriously. His habit of referring to them as "Mr." or

the courageous heart

"Miss" was too much. They ridiculed him for it constantly. He told them it was a sign of respect.

It was the hardest year of teaching he had ever experienced, and although he had put everything he had into it, signs of progress and rewards were few. One afternoon, during the last period of a very long and difficult day, he overheard one of the boys make an extremely crude and suggestive remark to one of the girls. It wasn't that he hadn't heard it before. Maybe it was because the school had no air conditioning and he was hot, maybe it was because he had a splitting headache, maybe he was just tired and fed up – it's hard to say –

but he reacted.

"Mr. Hutchens, I am sick of your filthy mouth. I want you to stand up right now and apologize to Miss Devore."

It was quiet; Mr. Hutchens did not move. He stared at the teacher with unbelief and defiance. He had never apologized to anyone in his life, and to do so under these circumstances would be a tremendous loss of face. He remained in his seat.

"Mr. Hutchens," the teacher rose from his desk and moved to the row the boy was sitting in. His growing anger made his voice dangerously quiet – almost a whisper – and he was trembling. He was conscious of two opposing things simultaneously. First, he wished he had not made a public issue out of this, and second, he was glad he had and he didn't care. "Mr. Hutchens, I told you to stand up – and *I mean it!*"

Mr. Hutchens remained seated, glaring insolently. The teacher grabbed him by his shirt front and jerked him to his feet. The boy's legs hit his desk, and it turned over with a terrible crash, spilling books and papers everywhere. A girl in the next row bent to pick them up. "Leave them where they are Miss Johnson. Mr. Hutchens will pick them up *after he has apologized.* Now, Mr. Hutchens, I – am – waiting – for – your – apology – to – Miss – Devore, and I will not wait very long." He was spitting the words out, and his anger was out of control.

"Miss Devore?" the boy chuckled with an emphasis on the "Devore." "Don't you mean Miss De_____?" He used a rhyming, common, vulgar expression for girls with loose morals. The class erupted in laughter, and he looked at the embarrassed and angry girl with an arrogant, triumphant smirk.

The teacher still had the boy's shirt grasped firmly in his left hand, and using that grip for leverage, he jerked the boy toward him and slapped him. He slapped him with every ounce of strength and energy he could muster – slapped him right across that smirking, sneering, defiant mouth. His thumb must have caught the boy's nose, or it may have simply been the tremendous impact, but the boy's nose began to bleed profusely, and there was a thin trickle of blood in the corner of his mouth.

The blow was so powerful that it stunned the boy. Angry red welts sprang to the surface of his face immediately, and he staggered and would have fallen if the teacher hadn't held him up. The only sounds in the classroom were whispers of awe and admiration from those who were impressed by the force of the blow.

The teacher's anger and resentment were quickly replaced with crushing disappointment. He marched the student – still groggy and struggling with his equilibrium – to the principal's office, seated him, explained briefly to the school secretary, and returned to his classroom. The low, excited buzz that had begun when he left was silenced at his return. He righted the desk, picked up the books and papers, and tried to return to the lesson. Fortunately, the period ended almost immediately. The students rushed into the halls to spread the news, and he went back to the principal's office to call the boy's parents and to explain in greater detail.

The principal was understanding and supportive. The boy's father came immediately, and when he heard the story, he told the teacher he wouldn't have any problems from him, that his son had gotten exactly what he deserved, and that he hoped it would teach him a lesson.

The teacher had thought it would certainly cost him his job. He knew it had already cost him something of far greater value – his self-respect and much of what he had for all these weeks been trying to teach – that Jesus makes us different. In this school, his action was much admired by the students. They spoke of the force of the blow with awe and respect in their voices – "Did you see Dick's head snap back when he hit him? It looked like he hit him with a brick." They thought more of their teacher because he had reacted *according to their standards of manhood* – "never take anything off of anybody."

He went home utterly defeated.

It came to him that night what he must do. He called the principal and asked him to call a school assembly the next day at noontime.

The teacher stood in the gym before a quiet, solemn student body and made a very sincere apology – not just to Mr. Hutchens, but to the faculty, the principal, and to every student whom he thought he had disappointed. He asked the forgiveness of all. When he finished, he walked toward the bleachers, his shoulders slumped, his heart heavy with failure. There was a stirring among some of the students, and from the crowd came Mr. Hutchens. He and the teacher met about half way across the floor; the boy was close to tears. They shook hands, and then the boy turned to his fellow students.

"I want to apologize to Mr. Jones. What I did was wrong, and what he did was right." He paused; he was trying to work up to something, and it was tough. "I want to apologize also to Nan – Miss Devore. I'm sorry I said what I did, and I want her to forgive me." The student body stood and cheered and applauded.

The healing seemed to melt and run through the whole school. It became the "in" thing to call everybody "Mr." or "Miss." Many good-natured jokes and much goodwill came from it.

There is healing and power in humility, in foot washing, in going the extra mile, in self-sacrifice, and in turning the other cheek.

> *"If any man would come after me,*
> *let him . . . take up his cross*
> *and follow me."*

His way is never easy,
but it is always best.

reflections . . .

reflections . . .

_____

_____

_____

_____

_____

_____

_____

_____

_____

_____

_____

_____

_____

121